Forew

Creating a Cookbook

How to Write, Publish, and Promote Your Culinary Philosophy

Amy Riolo

Copyright © 2018 Amy Riolo
All rights reserved

Published by Write Away Books
ISBN: 9781720009412

To Sheilah Kaufman with much love—
for teaching me to write cookbooks and much, much more.

Other Books by Amy Riolo

The Italian Diabetes Cookbook; Delicious and Healthful Dishes from Venice to Sicily and Beyond. Alexandria, VA, American Diabetes Association, 2016

The Ultimate Mediterranean Diet Cookbook; Harness the Power of the World's Healthiest Diet to Live Better, Longer. Boston, MA, Fair Winds Press, 2015

The Mediterranean Diabetes Cookbook – (Nautilus Award Winner) Alexandria, VA, American Diabetes Association, 2011

Nile Style; Egyptian Cuisine and Culture – (World Gourmand Award Winner) New York, NY, Hippocrene Books, 2013

Arabian Delights; Recipes & Princely Entertaining Ideas from the Arabian Peninsula. Washington, DC, Capital Books, 2007

Contents

Foreword 1

Introduction 3

Chapter One: Finding Your Niche in Food Writing 17

Chapter Two: Building an Author Platform 23

Chapter Three: How to Write a Recipe 31

Chapter Four: Writing a Cookbook Proposal 39

Chapter Five: Legal Issues: Agents, Contracts, and Copyrights 49

Chapter Six: Publishing: Self-Publishing vs. Traditional 57

Chapter Seven: Compiling a Cookbook 65

Chapter Eight: Cookbook Promotion 73

Suggested Reading/Resources 83

Acknowledgements

Destiny is to thank for enabling me to meet my cookbook mentor, Sheilah Kaufman, and to be able to publish my books in the first place. There is no direct path for cookbook authors, therefore the role of a good mentor is invaluable. I would probably never have published a cookbook if it weren't Sheilah, who patiently taught me much more than I ever planned on learning. I am proud to pass her knowledge and my experiences on to others.

There are scores of people around the globe who have given me writing and publishing tips that enabled me to achieve my objectives. I am fortunate to have been able to work with so many amazing writers and chefs, and to know them at such an intimate level. I believe that it truly "takes a village" to make a good chef and a good writer—and in my case, that village is a global one. I am honored and proud to say that I have learned from amazing cooks, authors, and publishers in places that I never dreamed I would even visit. For all of you who have shared a kitchen, a meal, or a good read with me, I thank you.

My nonna, Angela Magnone Foti, taught me to cook and bake, as well as how to use cookbooks, and other valuable lessons that served me outside of the kitchen. Because of her and our heritage, my first tastes of "Italian food" were Calabrian. Those edible time capsules formed a culinary bloodline between us and our relatives in southern Italy. Nonna Angela gave me my first cookbook and showed me how cooking was not a mundane chore, but a form of magic that could unite people across distance and time. I owe my career to her, and would give anything to be able to share more time in the kitchen with her. Cooking was so important to her that a few weeks before she passed away, at ninety years old, she refused to go into the hospital because it was Christmastime and she told the doctors that she needed to be home so that she could "make cookies with her granddaughter." It is an honor for me to be able to pass her knowledge on to my readers, and to inspire them to pass down their own family traditions through cookbooks.

My yia yia, Mary Michos Riolo, shared her beloved Greek traditions with me, and I am happy to say that they have become woven into my culinary fabric as well—especially since many Italian regions were Greek colonies in antiquity. My earliest memories of cooking were with my mother, Faith Riolo, who would sit me on the counter and roll more meatballs and cookies than I could count. She taught me that food was not just something we eat to nourish ourselves, but an edible gift that could be given to express love. When she assigned me with the "chore" of cooking as a teenager, it fueled my interest in cookbooks, and I began writing them to meet her dietary needs.

I owe my love of food history and anthropology to my father, Rick Riolo, for planting the desire to answer the question, "I wonder how they eat . . ." in my mind since childhood. It's a type of culinary curiosity that is never completely satisfied and gives me the motivation to continue my work each day.

I am very thankful to my partner, Chef Luigi Diotaiuti, for being a continuous source of inspiration and motivation, and for sharing my passions for maintaining culinary traditions that are on the verge of being forgotten and for always believing in my talent.

Thank you to Dr. Norton Fishman, Dr. Beth Tedesco, and Dr. Mary Lee Esty for enabling me to overcome my illness and fulfill my dreams. To my dear friend and confident, Susan Simonet. I don't know where I would be without your support. I am deeply grateful to my "Leading Light" Monica Bhide, for being such an amazing friend and inspiration. There are no words to express the heartfelt thanks that I feel for Kathleen Ammalee Rogers, who has been a faithful friend, talented healer, and adopted sister for many years.

I would like to thank Sedrick Crawley for helping me to clarify my career goals and to L'academie de Cuisine for giving me the opportunity to teach the How to Write a Cookbook series. Many thanks to Shawn Wenner, founder of *Entrepreneurial Chef* magazine, for featuring my "Cookbook Corner" column, which inspired this book, in his magazine. I would also like to thank Rossella Rago, Jane Graf, Ale Gambini, Clare Pelino, Nancy Baggett, and Keith Ogorek for sharing their knowledge, experience, and insights. Special thanks to my talented friend Lisa Comento for the book illustrations as well.

Foreword

Ah, the lure of an enticing cookbook . . . there really is nothing quite like it: peering at beautiful pages of alluring food, reading about tastes and temptations from lands far away, attempting to create a dish from the author's memorable experience. Cookbooks beguile us to do all this and more.

As a food writer and coach, the number one request I receive is: *"I have an idea for a cookbook, I have all these recipes, but I don't know what to do or where to start! Can you help me?"* In fact, the requests have been so frequent, I started teaching live seminars on the topic—but to attend, you had to be in Washington, DC, on the right day and at the right time.

Amy Riolo has created a guide that can help you when you are ready, anytime, anywhere!

She has created much more than a DIY model for someone who wants to create and publish their own cookbook. Yes, this will help you write the book you so dearly want to write. But more than that, it is a passionate guide that shows you how to do it effectively, efficiently, and season it with joy.

Her experience is par excellence. She is a best-selling author with a terrific platform. Yet that is just one of the attributes that make her the perfect person to write this book. What really stands out is her devotion to her art and her craft. I have never seen anyone work harder to create delightful cookbooks, and then teach the art of cooking and writing with such purposed intent and infectious passion.

Let this book guide your way. Read it from beginning to end before attempting to start writing. Then, once you have a sense of where you want to go, you can sit down and create a plan. Amy will show you the way!

My best to Amy and to all of you. May you always be blessed with memorable meals!

With relish,
Monica Bhide

Introduction

"There is no greater agony than bearing an untold story inside of you."
Maya Angelou

Cookbooks are so essential to my sense of personal well-being, that if I am not writing, or thinking about writing one, I feel that there is a huge void in my life. Writing, reading, and creating cookbooks is one of my greatest satisfactions. To me, cookbooks, even in their simplest form, have always been more than a collection of recipes. I began writing menus and developing recipes as a young child. It was my way of not only documenting the happiest moments in our family's life, but of anticipating more to come. Later on, as I learned that some of my most treasured dishes never had their recipes recorded, I made it my life's work to preserve them. I also had a strong desire to record "new" recipes which I began making to ensure that my family and friends could enjoy delicious food while maintaining optimal wellness.

Cookbooks give us the opportunity to pass down culinary and cultural patrimonies to future generations. They enable us to tell our personal stories in sensual terms that can be understood and appreciated by all. Cookbooks promote the pleasures of the table, the art of communication, the importance of family, and the science of good nutrition. Writing a cookbook was my way of entering the culinary arts. By the time I was twenty, I had a vast collection.

When I decided to write and publish my first book, however, I had no idea how to do it. I imagined if I had majored in journalism or writing—and also studied the culinary arts—I would have been better prepared. But truth be told, there really are no fields of study that prepare aspiring cookbook writers for what they will face as they set out to create their first book. Writing degrees, communication skills, and talent in the culinary arts are extremely helpful, but even those three subjects combined won't guarantee a successful or effective cookbook.

When I started out over a decade ago, the only true obstacle that I perceived to be in my way was getting published. I had ten years of research on my subject, strong communication skills, a passion for my topic, and lots of great recipes. Nonetheless, I had no idea how to take my manuscript and get it out there in the world. As I researched literary agents and pitched my ideas aimlessly to whichever publishers would accept unsolicited manuscripts, I decided to educate myself. I began taking food writing seminars and courses on how to publish books. I remember one of them in particular, because it was held at the Smithsonian Resident Associates Program. The registration fee for the event was costly for a budding writer, but the session featured a panel of very notable writers and food writing coaches. The catalogue description said that the seminar would cover cookbook writing and publishing, so I signed up right away.

Throughout the session, food writers gave their opinions and told stories about their careers. We were handed a sheet full of descriptive words to use, and some candies were passed out, so that we would learn how to best describe food. Very little information on how to publish a cookbook was given. That was my main objective for attending. When the seminar ended, I got in line and waited my turn to speak with the moderator, who was a food writing coach. I told her that I was new to the industry, that I had changed careers, and I desperately wanted to get my manuscript (which I printed out to show her and was holding in my hand) published. She took one look at me and the manuscript, and laughed. Then she proceeded to

INTRODUCTION

say, "If you want to make a career out of food writing, my suggestion is to find a patron or marry rich."

Needless to say, I was devastated. I wasn't asking for a get-rich strategy, just sound advice on how to get my book published. That day, I swore that if I ever did publish anything, I would teach others what I learned. I believe that the universe is ample. Even if every person on the planet wrote five cookbooks, there would still be room on the market for mine. Cookbooks are much more than just collections of recipes; they are our stories, our heritage, our memories, and guardians of all that we hold dear. While there would be some overlap in recipes if everyone wrote cookbooks, the style and the information that is shared would vary due to everyone's own unique human traits.

It is for this reason that I began writing the "Cookbook Corner" column for *Entrepreneurial Chef* magazine. I also began teaching courses on How to Write a Cookbook at L'academie de Cuisine, where I led recreational cooking classes in Bethesda, MD. This series is the first non-cooking or wine series that the school has offered. When I first created it, some of the other instructors thought it was odd that I would be teaching others how to do the same thing I do, and therefore create more competition in my field. But I don't see it that way. I look forward to reading everyone else's food stories as much as I enjoy sharing my own. I derive so much joy from writing cookbooks! I shudder to think of other newcomers trying their hardest and getting the same response that I did, and that is why I decided to do this.

Not too long after my negative experience at the food writing seminar, I realized that in order to learn the ropes of cookbook writing, I would need a mentor. I began affirming to myself (under my breath, of course) that "I have a wonderful mentor, and finding her will be easy." A few weeks later, I gave a lecture at the Egyptian Embassy in Washington, DC, on how the three monotheistic faiths shaped the cuisine of Egypt. Sheilah Kaufman came up to me and introduced herself as the food editor for a famous publication. She said that she had written twenty-six cookbooks, and would love to get me started. We became friends and she taught me the ropes. This book is dedicated to her, and she and her partner Paula Jacobson now have a company called The Cookbook Construction Crew, should anyone need their services.

To write and publish a cookbook of value, one must learn to evaluate the current market and analyze what is already available as well as what is needed. Hours, days, and months of research, recipe testing, and editing are involved. Because the cookbook market is such a competitive one, it is important to do the best job that you can. With the tips and practices mentioned in this book, you can put my experience as well as the experience of my colleagues to work for you. When you share your culinary philosophy with others, you are sharing a major part of yourself, and doing so can be an extremely rewarding experience. May you enjoy the process as much as I do! And may the creation of your cookbook open you up to a whole new delicious world!

All the best,
Amy Riolo

INTRODUCTION

Cookbook Writing – It's More Than Just Ingredients

An Essay by Jane R. Graf
US Group Sales Director
Casemate Group, Casemate Publishers, Casemate Academic, Casemate IPM, Casemate Art

As someone who has been in the publishing world for over thirty years, I've had the good fortune to work with some incredible authors, and the misfortune to know authors who manage to do all the wrong things and therefore lose sales and their reputations. To be successful takes full-time devotion to your craft, attention to the tiniest of details, and impeccable timing.

For cookbook authors, that is especially true, as inattention to details—from incorrect measurements or temperatures, to writing about an abandoned food trend—will cause more than your soufflé to fall!

So, let us look at a few of these important details. Whether you have a traditional publisher, or plan to self-publish, these details are critical, and you don't want to rely on someone else to do what is best for your book.

Finding the Right Publisher

If you are looking to publish a cookbook with a traditional publisher, either in print or electronic form, you must do your research and follow their requirements. First, look for a publisher who publishes cookbooks. Okay, that sounds like a ridiculous statement, but throughout my career, I've seen potential authors submit a manuscript to publishers who don't even work in that field. I had a local individual submit a cookbook manuscript recently to a nautical publisher. The cover letter read that as long as the individual lived down the road from the publisher, she thought they should publish her cookbook.

You want to take time to research what publishers work in the cookbook area, what types of cookbooks they produce, and what their requirements are for manuscript submission.

If a publisher produces heart-healthy cookbooks and you have a high-fat (but delicious!) desserts cookbook, they might not be the right publisher for you! If you are writing a soup book, you don't want to offer it to a grilling publisher.

Once you have selected the publisher(s) to whom you want to submit your book proposal, follow their directions for submissions *precisely*. If they want a fifty-word summary, a table of contents and one recipe—that is ALL you submit to them. Publishers are truly overwhelmed with book submissions, and can therefore afford to be picky. I know publishers who receive 200 submissions *per day*, but only end up looking at four to five of them, because the others didn't follow the submission guidelines.

Please note, some publishers will accept a submission proposal directly from an author, which is called "over the transom," whereas others only accept them via an agent. Do not try to trick a publisher into thinking you are an agent (or having a spouse or child represent themselves as your agent). Publishing is a small enough industry that a good editor knows all the agents in their field, and they share knowledge of "non-agented submissions" with one another.

Under Contract

When your proposal is accepted, your new publisher puts you "under contract." Congratulations! This means you will sign their contract, which will spell out precisely what they expect from you. READ IT CAREFULLY! You will be expected to follow the timeline laid out in the contract to the letter, and without reminders from their editorial team.

INTRODUCTION

Book publishing is at once a quick moving process—*we need your finished manuscript in four weeks!*—to one that moves at a glacial speed from getting your contract signed to seeing that finished book on the shelf at your local store or listed on the dot com of your choice. On average, it takes twelve to eighteen months for a book to go from proposal to finished product.

You will be scrambling to get your part completed on deadline, wait for editorial comments and corrections, and then scramble to get those corrections back to your editor—sometimes multiple times. You may, or may not, be given input on the interior layout, recipe images, or the cover design, depending on the publisher.

If your publisher asks you to provide photos for the book, which many will do, you don't want to take a snapshot with your phone of your dish and submit that. This is the time to get a professional photographer who understands composition and will make your recipe look its finest. In fact, whether you are publishing your book through a publisher or doing it yourself, the images within the book are crucial. Most readers pull the book off the shelf and flip through it, and your images are what grab their attention and will sell them on your book. Take the time and spend the money on a professional!

Once the manuscript is polished to perfection, the book goes into production. You'll have some downtime, but the publisher's sales and marketing team will be starting their efforts on behalf of your book. Be prepared to complete author questionnaires, prep for any promotions they might have planned, and practice your recipes until you can create them in the midst of all manner of distractions and chaos.

When the book is officially published, you will be its best advocate and ambassador. While a publisher takes on the financial burden of getting a book created and published in physical form, authors are the ones who truly bring their book to life. So talk up your book to everyone and every group you know. Stop at your local bookstore, tell them about your book, and offer to do a cooking demo and signing for their store. Offer to do one for your church, your alumni association, or other groups you might belong to. If there is a local food festival, talk to the organizer about taking a table, so you can pass out food samples, give away a recipe, and sell your book yourself. You are the one person who can bring your book to life, so don't hesitate to put yourself and your book out in front of an audience! How well that book sells, and how well it is reviewed, will determine if you'll be offered a contract for another book, so use it as your calling card wherever you go!

Self-Publishing

Should you opt to go the route of self-publishing, either in print or digital format, you need to recall that every detail that a publisher would regularly "handle" now fall into your hands. So make a list, and get ready to tick off a lot of items. You are now both an author and a business person, and the business is nearly always the more important half of that equation when you are a self-publisher.

I've tried to keep these in the order they need to be accomplished, putting the ones that can take the most time up front.

Your Publishing Company

When you opt to self-publish, you are now more than just an author; you are a publisher as well. That means you need to decide on a company name, get that company registered as a publisher with your state business association, and get a business license. You will also need to create a logo for your company, again one that you can live with for years to come. Ask a good graphic artist to create your logo; you want it to be professional, and one that will look good on the spine of your books as well. Get at least a basic website set up as well, one that is simple to work with that you can grow in the months and years ahead.

INTRODUCTION

ISBNs

Every book, no matter what format, has a unique ISBN or International Standard Book Number. This unique number allows anyone around the globe to find your book in stores or online, because as we all know there are plenty of books with the same title; *Cooking with Apples* may be the title, but the ISBN for the hard cover, paperback, and e-books all have a unique ISBN (yes, there are at least four versions of every e-book). Once you have your publishing company named, registered, and licensed, you will want to order your ISBNs. You need to do this at the very beginning of your process, before the book is even finished being written!

Bowker is the official provider of ISBNs, and you can go to their website to get your ISBNs: http://www.isbn.org/. You can opt to buy as many as you need for just your first book (in as many formats as needed), or you can purchase them in larger quantities, so that you can get a general "prefix" assigned to your company. Bowker makes it very easy to do, so work with the website, or call them to be walked through the process.

Pricing

Long before you are ready to print your book, you need to have mentally calculated the page count, determined how many recipes and images will be in it, whether the images are to be black and white or color, and talked to printers about costs to print your book. Most traditional printers, realizing all the costs they will put into the book (sales, marketing, shipping, review copy mailings, sales reps, etc.) take the book's printing unit costs and multiply that by either five or six times to come to the book's suggested retail price. So, for example, you have told the printer your book will be 120 pages, with color images throughout, it will be a hard cover, and will measure 7" x 9." The printer will come back to you with paper options, end papers, cover weights, and more, and will work with you to hammer out all the details.

CREATING A COOKBOOK

The printer will then give you their total cost to print the number of copies you've ordered. Say you ask for a 1,000-copy print run, and the printer tells you your total cost will be $2500 to print and ship the books to you. What that tells you is the cost of each book, or your unit cost, is $2.50 each. If you multiple that by five, it comes to $12.50; if you multiple that by six, your retail price would be $15.

The other thing to look at when pricing your book is what similar books are retailing for in the market. You have to think about similar topics, similar formats and size, and compare yourself to another author of similar experience. For example, if you're writing a French cookbook, comparing your book to a book by Jacques Pepin likely isn't fair, as his books sell in the tens of thousands, and therefore the books' unit costs will be much lower for his publisher. Remember, you can always increase the price of your books as your sales increase, you gain a solid reputation, and you see national demand for your books.

Library of Congress, LCCN

The United States Library of Congress is very interested in your book! It's true! They are so interested that as a publisher, you need to talk with them and get your LCCN, or Library of Congress Control Number. Your book needs to have one. Start here to apply for one: https://www.loc.gov/publish/pcn/. This is what you find on the inside front pages of a book with all your other bibliographic data. Don't believe me? Open up any book on your shelf and look at those opening pages. All that information is unique to every book, and will need to go into your front matter as well.

Copyright

When you write a book, the effort, words, and recipes are all yours, and belong to you. However, without a copyright on the book, anyone else can lift large sections of the book, or even the entire book, and publish it on their own as their own work. Or a store can copy it and sell it on their own. So start by looking at the government's copyright office at https://www.copyright.gov/ to understand what you need to do. Do some online research on copyrights and then get a lawyer to file the necessary paperwork for you. You want to be fully protected.

Writing the Book

You never thought I'd get here, did you? Being an author is one thing, but as a publisher as well, you have a lot to do before you can feel the freedom to write. But now it is time for you to really write your cookbook. Remember you need to reach your audience, so don't just type out a recipe you love; tell the story behind the recipe, talk about why it is nutritious, or tastes good, or why Uncle Ted always asks you to make this recipe for him when he visits. You want your recipes to come to life on the page, long before someone else goes shopping for the ingredients. In an ideal world, you want every recipe to start and finish on the same page, with perhaps a photo opposite the recipe. Think about it, you've just massaged brine into your turkey; do you really want to have to turn the page to find out what to do next?

As any chef will tell you, and as you know from your own kitchen experiments, creating a recipe is one thing, but perfecting it is something completely different. So, make your recipes multiple times. Does it change at altitude or at sea level? Does adding salt to the dish during cooking make a difference, or should you wait until you are about to serve it? If you are halfway into a recipe when you realize you don't have an ingredient, what can you substitute? You need to know these things to make the recipe divine, but your readers also want to know such things. So, add it to your story!

Editing, Design, and Layout

As an author and self-publisher, you need to be passionate about your food, but also dedicated to getting the language and the layout exactly correct. This is incredibly hard to do when you have written the book you are trying to edit and design. I highly recommend hiring a professional editor and designer to make your book look as good as your recipes taste. How many times have you read a book and found spelling and punctuation errors, or even had a character's name change halfway through the book? This is where someone who isn't personally invested in the book becomes incredibly helpful to have!

Yes, there are publishing software programs available, but even using those, too many books end up looking like you typed it up on your dad's old typewriter and took it to the local copy shop to have it printed and bound. There's nothing wrong with that if you just want to collect the family recipes to share at the holidays with your cousins. But if you truly want to be a publisher and an author with a gorgeous finished product that you would be proud to see in your local store's cookbook section, then hire the professional.

The same holds true for your images/photographs throughout the book. Hire a professional photographer, have them shadow you in the kitchen and take those great pictures, both while you are making your recipe, and of the finished product. Cell phone photographs, or even your friend's snapshots of you, are not what you want or need in your cookbook.

If your book is a digital one, you'll need to learn how to get it converted from your printed files, how many formats (and unique ISBNs) you'll need for each, and eventually how to get it listed on Amazon.com, barnesandnoble.com, and all your local and regional store's websites. Each website may need the book in different formats, or even multiple formats, to give their customers the best choices to purchase your book that is suitable for their phone, tablet, or computer. There are companies out there who can convert your typed version of the cookbook into a text-flowing e-book with the images placed correctly.

Replacing Your Chef's Toque with Your Salesman's Cap

After you've written the book and had it professional edited, designed, and photographed, you'll send it off to the printer and dream of the finished

INTRODUCTION

product. Once the printer delivers all those finished books to your home, you're allowed to get excited and call all your friends and family.

But recall, your work has only just begun. Now your toque comes off, and your salesman's cap goes on. You are in charge of selling the books to others, sending them out for review, and marketing yourself as a cookbook author. No doubt you'd rather be back in the kitchen, but if you want others to know about your book, as a self-publisher there is only one person to rely upon—*yourself*. You need to walk into every single bookstore and cooking store in your region. The book goes with you when you travel, so you can take it into the stores there. Online food bloggers, magazines, and other chefs all need to learn about your book, and you are by far its best salesman.

Your cookbook is now your calling card and entry into the world of sales!

Chapter One
Finding Your Niche in Food Writing

"Food is our closest connection to nature and the greatest employer on Earth, so valuing it properly represents our best hope of leading perpetuating, worthwhile, meaningful lives. Best of all, since food is our most reliable source of joy, we may as well follow Epicurus' advice and take pleasure in all it brings. By prizing food as a substance and a metaphor, we can build the foundations of a good life."

Carolyn Steel

There are over 3,000 cookbooks published in the United States alone each year. Being a great chef, owning a successful restaurant, and being an amazing writer are not guarantees to their success. Throughout my career, I have noticed how the most successful cookbook authors develop unique niches that work the best for them. I am speaking specifically to the idea of the author having a niche—not the particular title. That's another story, which we will discuss in "Chapter Four: Writing a Cookbook Proposal." With the advent of self-publishing, of course, you can publish any idea without thinking about your niche, or the book's, but if you want your efforts to pay off and to pave a long-standing culinary career for yourself, it is much better to think of these things in the beginning.

Even if you're writing your first book and don't plan on writing another, you should identify a unique position in the market which will allow you to market yourself and your work effectively. Think about talks that you would like to give and panels that you would like to be a part of. Which topics would you be most excited sharing with the media, or telling on television? The answers will help you to identify what is most important to you—the message that you have to give.

Once you pinpoint your message, a little bit of competitive market analysis will help you determine what is in demand. If there are a lot of titles with ideas similar to yours, for example, that is a wonderful thing. Your job is then to position your unique, and hopefully better, easier, or more fun take on that popular genre. If there are no other ideas in the market similar to yours, it will be hard to sell, because people will feel it is not needed. In order to be successful, you need to find your most marketable strengths and marry them with topics that are in demand.

For many people, defining a "niche" can be the most difficult part of writing a cookbook. I've heard a lot of chefs describe their food as their unique position within the market. For example, someone might say that a certain culinary culture is their niche. But I suggest being much more specific than that for a few reasons. First of all, the particular culture does not belong only to you. Even if you represent a food culture that is "new on the scene," you will soon be joined by peers. The second reason is that most of the media contains one "box" per culture. If you are an Italian, French, or Spanish chef who brands yourself as such, you will always be competing for that one box. When I was starting out, for example, a lot of my work got turned down because magazines and book publishers told me that they already had "Italian chefs" and "Italian stories." So, I realized that I had to literally think outside of that box. I learned that if you develop your niche in other ways, such as marrying a unique combination of strengths and passions along with a market demand, you will ensure success for years to come.

The best way to illustrate my point is probably to use myself, once again, as an example. When I first starting writing cookbooks, the word "niche" was the last thing on my mind. I had such a deep desire to get published that I could not see beyond my first book title. I built a strong author platform specifically to get that one book published, never dreaming that I would write more than that. Before the first book was even published, however, I was already working on cookbooks number two and three. It wasn't until well after my fourth book that a PR person told me, "Your niche is the 3 H's...that's where you live." By the three H's, she meant "History, Home, and Health," because at the core of my work, you will find those common elements—food history and lots of health-related information along with how people can interpret the recipes and recreate particular culinary cultures in their own home. For years I had incorporated those elements without ever giving them a thought. By not knowing this niche from the beginning, I missed out on a lot of opportunities because I believed my niche was culture. Those three topics, however, are what I am most passionate about, and what I do best. Fortunately, they also transcend culture, so I am able to write about many places. I am not the only author to discuss "the three H's," but the theme is at the core of my philosophy, and it is also of need and interesting to the public, so I stick with it.

Let's forget about cookbooks for a second. Think about other kinds of books, such as those written by Nora Roberts or Stephen King. Can you imagine if they switched their niches? A romance by Stephen King and a thriller from Nora Roberts probably wouldn't fare so well on the market—not because those authors can't write them, but because they have some of the strongest niches on the bestseller list, and they know what the world wants from them.

Many of my colleagues come to me when defining their niches for various blogs, books, or brands. Over the years, I have enjoyed helping many people identify the strengths which have the most marketability. One of my assistants, Ed Donnelly, for example, has a great deal of knowledge in molecular gastronomy. He has the potential to define himself as such, but there are already many culinary greats specializing in that particular part of the industry. Because we work together, I noticed that not only does he have an affinity to molecular gastronomy, but he's a genius at finding really easy, inexpensive ways for people to create highly sophisticated techniques at home. I label his niche as "Molecular Gastronomy Made Easy," because even though the field has stiff competition, few people break it down as easily as he does.

Once an intern of mine had the goal of writing a cookbook. I promised her that by the time she finished with me she would have a professional proposal together. She wanted to write about a particular country, which currently did not have a cookbook in English to represent it. My advice to her was to identify ways in which her nation had marketability. The fact that there is no one currently writing on that topic, to a business person, means that there is no interest. By highlighting the international appeal of the nation (in addition to its cuisine) and comparing it to nearby popular culinary territory, she was able to develop her idea. She came up with a concept (and consequently a mission) which enabled her to tell the story of her country through food and market the idea as a "next big thing" cuisine, which was drawing upon international notoriety and the fact that the country's food (which was similar to the popular cuisine of its neighbors) was begging to be explored. Her niche became promoting her country through its cuisine and vice versa.

Another friend of mine, Chef Matt Finarelli, came to me when he was about to write his first book. Matt is an Italian-American chef with a wide range of experience and a lot of talent. Matt was irked with the stereotype of "red sauce" and Italian food. His mission was to prove to the world that Italian cuisine had much more to offer. When working with Matt, I noticed that he also had a unique way of doing most standard professional chef "techniques." He even has his own way of chopping an onion, which is extremely efficient, and it is his "alternative" method that his students and staff learn to use. I coupled the idea of Matt's unique food philosophies and styles along with his passion for non-tomato-based Italian recipes and came up with the title *Beyond the Red Sauce* for his cookbook. I believe Matt will go on to create many great books and concepts. In staying true to his niche, it is important that each one of them make the reader think differently about the particular subject than they did before. That is his niche—it goes beyond ethnicity and style to evoke an emotion and prove his points.

As you can see, niches are highly individualistic. Determining a position in the market is imperative to success, and the process can be fun. If you haven't done so already, once you begin to focus on your niche, things will really fall into place. You can use them in social media, restaurant and menu promotions, and advertising as well.

Here are some points to consider:

1. Your personal niche may be different than that of your restaurant or place of employment. If you are writing a book on your own, then the niche can speak more to "your story," but if it is a branded book for the business, then it needs to tell both.
2. When deciding upon your niche, always think about your passions, talents, and strengths (especially those that others tell you about), and write them down.
3. Think about which of those things means the most to you.
4. Do some competitive market analysis by researching other chefs with similar attributes.
5. Decide what makes you unique compared to the competition.
6. Determine if the world would care about that difference—would they need to know?
7. If so, you have found a nice niche for yourself. Now all you have to determine is which topic you would like your first book to be about.

Voice

Just like with other books, the "voice" that you use in your cookbooks will help to reinforce the style of the book as well as your niche. Your choice of writing style, types of adjectives, and descriptors should speak to your demographic. The voice of a historically-inspired cookbook which features Victorian tea recipes should be written in a very different manner than a modern cookbook on barbecue or one on regional Indian cuisine.

If you are new to writing as a whole, familiarize yourself with food writing. Read as many types of food publications and culinary books as possible to recognize the various styles, tones, and voices that authors use. Once you begin to notice the patterns, you can begin to think about your own. You may already have a collection of recipes, or recipe titles, and stories together. Think about your own niche and the demographic whom you will be reaching with your book. Find the best way to represent your food with writing that matches its style and is interesting to read.

Chapter Two
Building an Author Platform

"Here's the thing: The book that will most change your life is the book you write."

Seth Godin

An author "platform" is the part of your biography or resume which is most synergistic to your book(s). Your platform is what will enable you to sell and promote your work. Nowadays, regardless of how you choose to publish your work, your platform is every bit as important as the book itself. It is the deciding factor which will make or break your deal with a publishing house. Even if you self-publish your book, prospective viewers will usually read your platform to determine your expertise on your subject prior to buying your work.

Constructing your platform is not difficult, but it can take time. If you are wondering what a "platform" is, flip to the back page or blurb about the author in your favorite cookbooks. Those sections usually reveal a short bio of the author. They may write for magazines or newspapers, teach cooking classes, hold culinary or journalism degrees, and belong to many food organizations and other professional organizations. Some cookbook authors are celebrities, restaurant chefs, or owners of a culinary brand. Others teach at universities or have complimentary titles such as sommelier, nutritionist, or dietician.

A powerful platform includes both information which highlights the author's expertise in the subject matter and reveals the multitude of ways in which they would be successful in selling tens of thousands of copies of their books. Your platform should make it clear that you are the perfect person to write your book. If you don't have all of these in place for your topic, it might be the wrong choice for you at this time. You can work on building expertise in that area while starting with a subject that you are very knowledgeable and skilled at.

So, if you are writing a book about gourmet, gluten-free cuisine, for example, it would be advantageous to have some kind of medical experience. Maybe you work for an organization which creates awareness for celiac disease or are a popular blogger in the gluten-free community who follows a gluten-free lifestyle. Maybe you're a doctor, a nutritionist, or a dietician who assists patients with the illness. You might even have first-hand experience in creating delicious, gluten-free recipes for your family, or if you are a professional chef, in your restaurants. These qualifications would all help your reader to view you as an expert in your field, and that will help to sell books.

On the other side of the equation is how your platform can reach a large audience to help you sell books. If you have a radio, TV, or internet show, or make frequent appearances on one, that would be wonderful. Writing a column on your subject and doing webinars on it would also help a great deal. If you have a brick and mortar store or restaurants in which you can sell your book, that would help as well. A large social media presence in your field of expertise is also extremely important. Giving lectures (especially those that are podcast) on your specialty also helps a great deal. I also highly recommend joining cultural organizations, sports clubs, alumni associations, community interest groups, and clubs of your choice. If these types of affiliations will enable you to mention your book in their newsletter or online, host book signings, or help you to promote in any other way, then they are more than worth the effort. There are also writers' groups in many cities which will help you to promote your work, and are a good option for new authors.

When I started to build my author platform, these are the things I focused on:

1. I joined as many professional culinary organizations that fit my philosophy as possible. I highly recommend the following, especially for newcomers:

- International Association of Culinary Professionals
- Slow Food
- Your city's local Culinary Historians group

2. I aligned myself with cultural organizations that were relevant to my heritage and the topics of my books. They included:

- The National Italian American Foundation
- The Italian Cultural Society
- The National Organization of Italian American Women
- Sister Cities International (I chaired the Baltimore-Luxor-Alexandria Sister City Committee)
- Welcome to Washington International
- The Hospitality and Information Services for Diplomats

3. I actively attended events at organizations which I would like to speak at—or contacted the events divisions directly. These now include:

- The Library of Congress
- Georgetown University
- Johns Hopkins University
- The US Endocrine Society (Culinary Stage at Annual Conference)
- National Geographic
- The International Visitors Center of LA
- The Italy America Chamber of Commerce

CREATING A COOKBOOK

- The Italian Cultural Institute
- The Utah Council for Citizen Diplomacy
- The Smithsonian Institution
- The International Visitors Center of Los Angeles
- The Fulbright Commission
- The National Museum of African Art
- The Textile Museum
- The Walters Art Museum
- The Kennedy Center
- Sharjah International Book Fair
- Sharjah Children's Reading Festival
- Abu Dhabi International Book Fair
- The Embassy of the Arab Republic of Egypt
- The Embassy of Yemen
- The Library of Alexandria (Egypt)

4. Because some of my books were diabetes-friendly, I became involved with:

- The US Endocrine Society
- The American Diabetes Association
- The Your Wellness program at Harris Teeter Supermarkets

5. I joined the following alumni associations:

- The Cornell University Entrepreneurial Network
- The Cornell Club of Washington

6. I taught and spoke on my topic everywhere I could, sometimes for free in the beginning. I also wrote articles and blogposts and hosted videos for free—just to build recognition and a platform. Here are a few good options:

For teaching and speaking:

- Local cooking schools
- Farmer's markets
- Local bookstores or cultural centers
- Religious organizations
- Private classes
- Schools

For writing:

- Ask to be a guest blogger on your favorite blog
- Write recipes or cooking information for a local newspaper or newsletter
- Join writing groups in your area
- Start, or continue writing your own blog
- It is always advisable for an author to blog—that way you can connect with your reader while creating a wider audience for your books

For videos:

- Create your own YouTube channel if you don't already have one
- Feature videos in which you are showcasing your expertise
- Promote your videos on social media
- Team up with budding production companies, video libraries, and videographers who are interested in building content and create some cooking videos with recipes that would be in your book

7. Become an expert in your field. If you are new to the industry, make some affiliations which will give you credibility. These may include:

- Degrees or certificates from accredited programs in your sector
- Accolades. Be nominated for awards or titles; if you win, that is an immediate boost to your platform
- Offer to speak on your topic at organizations and/or do webinars

8. Team up with brands and blogs

- Are there companies which are very complimentary to your book title or culinary philosophy? If so, reach out to them and see if they want to collaborate. You may get a great sponsorship deal, or, at minimum, the chance to cross-promote your book with their products.
- If you know of blogs which speak straight to your demographic, follow them, engage with them, and build a rapport. When your book comes out, you can ask them to mention it, do a giveaway, or write a review

To give you a specific example of what I am describing, and the time it takes to grow a platform, the following is my platform statement from the back of my first cookbook, which I wrote in 2007:

> "Amy Riolo is a nationally recognized[a] culinary expert, food writer[b], and cooking instructor in the Washington, DC area. She is a member of The International Association of Culinary Professionals, Les Dames d'Escoffier, Slow Food DC, Culinary Historians of Washington, Baltimore –Alexandria- Luxor Sister City Committee, Cornell Club of Washington, and Welcome to Washington International. She maintains a home in Egypt and travels to the region as[c] often as possible to keep abreast of Arabian culinary trends."
>
> [a] *I was not yet internationally known, it was my first book, so this is what they wrote.*
> [b] *I was not an author yet – so I used the term food writer*
> [c] *Since I am from a different culture than the one I was writing about, the publisher added this in to show my expertise in the area.*

When my last cookbook came out, this is what the back cover said:

"Amy Riolo is an award-winning author[d], chef[e], television personality[f], cuisine and culture expert, and educator[g]. She is best known for teaching about history, culture, nutrition, and diabetes-friendly eating through global cuisine. She makes frequent appearances on television and radio both in the US and abroad, including appearances on Fox, CBS, The Travel Channel[h], and Martha Stewart Living Radio. Her book *The Mediterranean Diabetes Cookbook* won the 2011[i] Nautilus Book Award. The Italian Diabetes Cookbook is her seventh[j] book.

[d] *By this time, I was published and had won awards*

[e] *I also had professional kitchen experience*

[f] *I hosted my own Culture of Cuisine Series*

[g] *I became s successful teacher and lecturer*

[h] *My TV experience increased*

[i] *I won other book awards as well – but this one was relevant to this publisher, so they listed it*

[j] *This shows that I have experience*

You can also flip to the back cover of this book to see the additional changes I have made since the last book and how they tie-in to writing a cookbook. If the topic of creating your platform seems daunting to you, begin slowly and take your time. Make meaningful connections in your field and align yourself with like-minded people and those who will support your ideas. If you stay true to your vision, it is amazing how quickly your platform will come together.

Chapter Three
How to Write a Recipe

"A cookbook is only as good as its poorest recipe."

Julia Child

The etymology of the word "recipe" hails from the Latin word *recipere* which means "to take" or "to receive." In sixteenth century England, the word receipt was used when describing a procedure for making a dish. In the last few hundred years, recipes have evolved greatly from simple lists of ingredients with very minimal instructions like the ones that I have handed down from my great-grandmother to the detailed, fool-proof versions we have instant access to today. Nowadays, well-written, easy to follow, interesting recipes are integral to successful cookbooks. If you're a chef, people assume you can write a recipe—but that's not always the case. Restaurant recipes are larger in scale and assume a great deal of culinary knowledge that the average home cook doesn't have.

Truth of the matter is, unless you've taken a course in recipe writing, you're probably doing it wrong. It's my observation that the best cooks need the most help initially, because they assume that the reader of the recipe is skilled in the kitchen. When I first started, for example, the instructions in one of my written recipes read: "roast the leg of lamb and then…" When my cookbook mentor, Sheilah Kaufman, who runs The Cookbook Construction Crew read it, she burst out laughing. I remember her saying, "Amy, not everyone knows how to roast a lamb! You must explain everything. And you have to write as if you were addressing a third grader." She later went on to say that you can never over-explain anything, because the painstaking details are needed by novice cooks. More savvy chefs, she added, will skip over the information they already know. The details will make the experience better for newcomers to the kitchen. Since I now write hundreds of recipes a year, I have streamlined the process a great deal.

Here are my steps:

1. Choose the recipe name

When I first started, I would translate popular international recipe names into English. One of my titles was Bread and Meat! After a while, it occurred to me that I should make them sound more appealing for readers who weren't familiar with the original recipe. In hindsight, Homemade Flatbread with Spice-Infused Lamb and Tomato Topping would have been more appropriate. Today, recipe titles need to sound great, be appetizing, accurately describe what they are, and respect origin if necessary.

In English, recipe titles are usually written with the first letter of each word (except prepositions) capitalized—such as Homemade Flatbread with Spice-Infused Lamb and Tomato Topping. In many other languages, just the first word of a recipe (if any) is capitalized. For example, in English we write Linguine with Clams, but in Italian only the first word is capitalized, so it's Linguine alle vongole.

Some editors prefer different styles, and you will always get a style sheet with a cookbook contract so that you can double-check. With digital recipes, and for social media purposes, it is highly advisable to choose recipe names keeping search engine optimization in mind as well.

2. Develop the header

Headers are the paragraph on top of the recipe. This is the chef or author's chance to explain the history of the recipe, its reason for being, or tell the story of who or how it came to be. The tone and subject of the header should be in harmony with the voice of your book. For example, if your cookbook is a memoir, then your headers should include personal stories about the particular food or recipe. If your slant is history or health–related topics, then your header should include that information.

Here is the header for one of the recipes in my *Ultimate Mediterranean Diet Cookbook*. Since I am a food historian, I discuss the history of the recipe, and since the book is health-related, I included that information. Note also the capitalization in the title.

Whole-Wheat Grape and Rosemary Focaccia/*Schiacciata all'uva*

> *Schiacciata*, the name of this delicious bread in Italian, is derived from the verb *schiacciare,* which means "flattened out" or "squashed"—and that's exactly what happens to the dough when freshly harvested grapes are pressed into it. Traditionally made at grape harvest time in Tuscany, this recipe is said to have originated with the Etruscans and was originally baked in the ashes of an open hearth. Luckily, it's simple to make and suits modern palates perfectly.

3. List the ingredients (in order of use in preparation)

Different publishing houses have different requirements for ingredients. Some of them ask that you write the word "ingredients" on top of the list; others don't. Some like to number recipes; others do not. Water is usually not listed in the ingredients unless it is a certain temperature. Some publishers require dual measurements, while others require only one. What is standard procedure, however, is listing the ingredients in the order that they will be used. Here is an example from the recipe mentioned above:

1 1/2 cups (355 g) warm water
1/2 cup (120 ml) Vin Santo (Italian dessert wine)
1 package (1/4 ounce, or 7 g) active dry yeast
1/2 cup (118 ml) extra-virgin olive oil, divided, plus extra for greasing pan
3 cups (375 g) whole-wheat flour (See Gluten-Free Alternative)
1 cup (125 g) unbleached, all-purpose flour (See Gluten-Free Alternative)
1 teaspoon unrefined sea salt or salt
2 cups (300 g) seedless red grapes, cut in half lengthwise

4. Write the preparation description in order and in detail

Once again, different publishers will have different guidelines. Some prefer the preparation section to be numbered and others do not. A few common pitfalls are:

- Not telling the reader where to put something (such as "combine ingredients and mix well"). Where do they combine them? What size bowl? What do they use to combine them—a wooden spoon or a whisk?
- Timing is also very important. How long does it take for something to cook, bake, or rise? What is the sensory indication that it is done (color, smell, feel, etc.)?
- Always include temperatures and times for cooking.

- Cooling, storing, and serving suggestions are integral.
- Always tell the servings of a recipe (how many people does it feed?).
- Some editors will ask for serving sizes (how large is each portion per serving?).
- Some editors will ask for cooking times (total vs. active).

Here is an example from the same recipe:

Pour the water and Vin Santo in the bowl of a standing mixer. Sprinkle the yeast over the top, and mix using the paddle attachment until combined. Let set for 5 minutes. Pour in 1/4 cup (60 ml) of olive oil. Add the whole-wheat flour and mix on low speed. Slowly add in the all-purpose flour and salt, and mix until well combined.

Switch to the dough hook attachment and knead the dough on medium speed for 5 minutes. Cover the bowl with plastic wrap and allow to rest at room temperature until doubled in size, about 1 hour.*

Oil a 13 x 17-inch (33 x 43 cm) rimmed baking sheet. Turn the dough out from the bowl onto the baking sheet. Using your hands, stretch the dough out and press down until it covers the surface of the pan in an even layer.

Using all the fingers of your hands, press down to make dimples in the surface of the focaccia. Cover with oiled plastic wrap and allow to rest for 30 minutes, or until the dough has doubled in size again.

Preheat the oven to 425°F (220°C).

Before baking, remove the plastic wrap and brush the surface of the focaccia with the remaining 1/4 cup (60 ml) of olive oil. Scatter the grapes, cut side down over the top and press them down slightly.

CREATING A COOKBOOK

Bake for 30 to 35 minutes, or until the focaccia turns a nice golden brown and is cooked through.

Remove from the oven and allow to cool slightly. Cut and serve immediately. Leftover, cooled pieces can be wrapped in plastic wrap and frozen for up to 1 month.

5. Consider offering a tip or technique that speaks to your brand

If the scope of your book is to de-mystify restaurant recipes for the home cook, then you should incorporate tips at the end of the recipe that give tricks of the trade that people can use at home. The book I am using as an example is on The Mediterranean Diet, so I wanted to give every recipe a Mediterranean Tradition:

> Mediterranean Tradition
> The challenge of preparing freshly harvested vegetables in as many ways possible is something that chefs and home cooks in the Mediterranean region take great pride in. Challenge yourself to go outside of your culinary comfort zone when your favorite fruits and vegetables are in season—you'll be sure to discover new favorites and increase your plant-based food intake.

Since home cooks can always use assistance with fitting cooking into their busy lifestyles, I also include other scheduling tips such as:

*If you would like to make this dough in the morning to eat in the evening, cover the bowl very well with plastic wrap and a clean kitchen towel and place in the refrigerator. In 12 hours, you will have the same results as if it sat at room temperature for 1 hour.

6. Test your recipes

Once you have your recipe written, you should take it back into the kitchen and use it as a guide to prepare the dish. Make notes and corrections as needed. In addition, I like to use this time to add in my descriptors. For example, if I tell people to mix for 5 to 7 minutes until smooth, this is my chance to witness what I am doing and come up with additional adjectives to describe what "smooth" really looks, feels, smells, or tastes like. I also set my timer and double-check my times. Then, I look for ways I can add more description about the speed that I am mixing at (low, medium, high, fast, slow, occasionally, etc.). I also make note of anything I left out.

7. Have other people test your recipes

There are professional and amateur recipe testers who will be happy to test your recipes out—some for a fee, others for a free book and some ingredients. I highly recommend having others who are not familiar with the recipe test it out, because their viewpoint will be more like the readers' than yours. I give testers a list of guidelines.

Recipe Testing Guidelines
Please complete this questionnaire for each recipe

*Recipe headers and procedures contain copyrighted material – please do not distribute

1. Were you familiar with this dish before trying the recipe?
2. If no, did the recipe header do an accurate job of describing it?
3. Was the recipe easy to follow?
4. Were the directions accurate and easy to understand?
5. Did you need to make any changes to the recipe?

6. Did anything need more clarification?
7. Can you think of a way to improve upon the recipe?
8. What did you like/dislike about the recipe?
9. Any additional comments?

Correct and Retest Recipe

Once I have the testers' feedback in hand, I correct the recipe where needed and make the necessary adjustments. If they suggest changes in the kitchen, I take the recipe back in and recreate the recipe to make sure it works. Then I go back to the recipe and change it another time.

Have Recipes Edited

Once you have done as much as you can with a recipe, hand it over to a professional recipe editor (preferably with a style sheet from your publisher in hand) and have them edit it. Then you can go back and make changes. At this point, you will have a professional recipe to hand in.

Chapter Four
Writing a Cookbook Proposal

"Write what should not be forgotten."

Isabel Allende

Think of a well-researched and carefully written proposal as the business plan of your book. Whether you are planning on self-publishing or going the traditional route, a professional proposal is an important part of the process. If you plan on submitting your proposal to a literary agent or directly to a publisher, making it as polished and thorough as possible helps you put your best foot forward. The proposal will enable the prospective agent or publishing house to understand your concept and determine whether or not it is a good fit for them. It will also reveal your writing style, voice, author platform, and business savvy.

Many people who self-publish think that they should skip over the proposal writing process because they are time consuming, but that's a mistake. Taking the time to write a proposal before crafting your book can help you to also determine its marketability and analyze the competition If you want to make money with your book, you should be every bit as cautious about going forward with the venture as a publishing house would. The process of developing the proposal will help you to tighten your own ideas, distinguish yourself from the competition, and set up a strong marketing platform (which we will discuss in a few months' time) that will help you to sell more books and get more publicity.

Below is a template for the type of format I use when writing a cookbook proposal. An explanation of each section is written underneath the boldface header. Note that various authors and publishers may use various templates, and some prefer different lengths. My proposals tend to be quite long, because I want to include as much information up front as possible. If you are ever asked to submit a shorter proposal, you can always edit it down.

Proposals are usually single-spaced and written in a traditional font, such as Times New Roman size 12. They contain a cover page with the name of the proposed book, the word "proposal," and the author's name, address, email, and date. If you are submitting to a publishing house, they may take up to three months to respond to you. Literary agents usually have their own policies, and may give you a timeline during your initial conversations with them.

This is what I recommend submitting:

Overview
This section is usually a page in length and gives an overall synopsis of the book's premise, why it is needed, and why the author is the best person to write it. It's important to begin the first paragraph with a compelling statement to get the reader excited about the concept.

Key Points
- This is a bullet-point list of the key factors (say five to ten) that your book offers.
- I usually include things like the number of recipes included, why the recipes are relevant, any unique factors about the book—in essence, the reasons why people would purchase it.

New Features

- This is another bullet-point or numeric list of features which are new in your book.
- For example, your book might be the first to demystify a certain type of cooking to English speakers, or it might be the first cookbook devoted to a certain area or technique. Whatever it is, you will want to outline that here.

Why Now?

This section is where you want to outline why this book is needed. You are illustrating its importance and marketability. Statistics are very helpful here. For example, if you can prove that there is a 50 percent increase in happy hour business in the United States as well as a significant increase in home entertaining, and your book is about DIY cocktails, mixology, or bar food, that would be beneficial. If there is a large, nationwide increase in any culinary trend or specific ingredient, it would also be great to mention it here. If your specific business also feeds the above-mentioned trend, then you could also speak to the trend from a place of personal authority which would make it even more compelling. You can research food associations, specialty food magazines, and supermarket trends to determine what is growing in popularity. If there is a need for more knowledge or DIY information regarding those trends, then your book will be even more relevant.

Marketing and Promotion

Many believe this section to be the backbone of the proposal. The days of the publisher doing all of the PR and marketing for cookbooks are gone. Nowadays, authors and publishers partner together to create winning strategies. At the end of the day, however, it is up to the authors to promote their own books. If you want to earn a significant amount of money doing so, then you cannot spend too much time on this section. A great deal of my personal schedule and resources are spent on marketing and promoting my books. The good news is that once you build up a platform, you can continue to use it for future books. I begin my marketing strategy long before writing my books.

My marketing elements will include:
This section reveals exactly what you plan to do in order to sell books.

Author-Driven Publicity: If you have access to media outlets—print, television, radio, and blogs—you can mention that you will pitch them with strategic press releases and concepts here. In addition, if you have secured a PR person, you want to mention them here. Not all publishing houses designate PR campaigns for all of their books, and having your own agent can be extremely helpful.

1. Social Networking and Web
Social networking will be a valuable tool for marketing your book. Here you want to say, "For the promotion of this book, I plan to do the following:" (These are a few of the ideas that my colleagues and I use to promote our books).

- Create _____ videos. They will be aired on: _____.
- Create a supporting Facebook page for the book, where readers will be able to find extended resources, up-to-date information, and discuss with the authors and other users via an online forum. The site will also include a blog, podcast, and speaking engagement calendar.
- Leverage Google AdWords, where we can drive users to the Facebook page.
- Utilize Facebook, Twitter, Instagram, and Pinterest for ongoing promotional purposes, where we will engage readers and announce book updates and speaking engagements.

Offer a "book ambassador" incentive to A-list bloggers to solicit reviews on their blogs and Amazon. These include:

- Along the tour, I will work with small, local restaurants, cultural centers, and food companies to plan book events, including menus based on recipes from the book. Locations may include:

- I plan to solicit television appearances with (I have already appeared on many of these shows and make television appearances frequently):
- I plan to solicit radio interviews with:

2. I also plan to solicit print reviews with contacts I have at:

3. Endorsements: The following experts are willing to endorse the book:

Competitive Works

This is my favorite part of the proposal. Here you want to pick three competitive titles, meaning that they are similar to your idea. If they are synergistic to your book, as well as best-sellers, those are the ones that you want to mention. Then, you write a few paragraphs comparing and contrasting the three other titles versus yours. You always want to first write a paragraph explaining what you have in common, and then a subsequent paragraph explaining why your book is even better. Perhaps it has more recipes, explains an idea further, or has additional features, or maybe you have more credentials on the topic than the competitive author. That is what you want to include in this section.

About the Author:

This is your author platform. A one to two-page bio explaining why you are the best person to write and market this book is what you want to include. "Chapter Two: Building an Author Platform" is dedicated to specifically to this topic. If you are having trouble getting started, take a look at the book jackets of other cookbooks, and you will get a feel for how authors are poised to be subject matter experts. If you are not a subject matter expert on this particular book, but the topic interests you greatly, I highly recommend beginning with a book that is in line with your expertise and then saving the original topic for a later publication.

Table of Contents

That's right, the complete table of contents is due at the time that you submit the proposal, complete with chapter names and recipe titles. Here's a rough example:

Introduction
Include a few sentences telling what your introduction will include.
Chapter One:
Give each chapter a title and briefly discuss what it will cover. You may have as many as you need. I only included four in the template.
Chapter Two:
Chapter Three:
Chapter Four:

Sample Chapter

You will need to submit one sample chapter. It may be the chapter of your choice. Some people choose the chapter to include based upon the popularity of its topic; others choose it for sentimental reasons. You may include whichever you like best. Since you will also include sample recipes, it may be advantageous to include the sample chapter introduction that corresponds with the recipes that you are submitting. For example, if you are submitting all dessert recipes, then that is the chapter that I would include as the sample. Even if your cookbook is a collection of recipes without a great deal of writing, each chapter will need an introduction. For example, the dessert chapter could have a page or two or three written about the types of desserts that you will feature in the chapter and why. Anecdotes, stories, health benefits (if applicable), history, and memories are all great to include in the chapter introductions.

Sample Recipes:

In this section, you will want to submit ten to fifteen well-written and professionally edited recipes. (See Chapter Three: How to Write a Recipe.) Also, make sure that the recipes you include are appetizing and that they have been professionally tested. Many editors will test the recipes of prospective authors before giving them contracts to ensure that they work. It is always a good idea to submit the most popular, on-trend recipes possible.

These are the basic requirements of proposal writing. While it can be frustrating in the beginning, once you get the hang of it, creating the proposal can be one of the most rewarding parts of your writing experience. Your next step will be to determine whom to submit the proposal to, and we will cover that in Chapter Six: Self-Publishing vs. Traditional.

CREATING A COOKBOOK

Coaching on a Cookbook Proposal

By Clare Pelino
President
Profile PR & Pro Literary

1. Research what's already been done on the subject—Amazon/local book store/blogs. Does someone else live in your space already?

2. Demonstrate that your point of view and the contents of the book will bring a different focus on the subject. Sometimes a subject is popular and the more that is said about that subject is often better.

3. How will your book bring more good information to the table? Or why is it needed? What do you have to say that it not quite out there yet?

    The most important part of a proposal is to give an editor a clear idea of the contents of your book. The editor cannot acquire the book otherwise.

4. The editor needs to be able to read your style of writing.

5. This is why a full chapter (typically Chapter 1) should be included.

6. There also needs to be a well-developed table of contents so an editor can envision the book.

7. There also needs to be a sampling of eight to ten recipes that have been tested.

8. Photography can be included if you have a clear vision of what you want the book to look like. They do not have to be the final photos that would be used in the book. They can be examples that offer the editor a better picture of what your food looks like or help the editor to envision the style you want.

9. I have encountered writers that feel like it's too much effort to do this work. I know that sounds crazy, but it happens. You will not get as good a deal if you don't do the work up front. Or, there is a chance that you may get overlooked altogether. Many editors don't acquire books without trying some of the recipes anymore.

10. At the same time, an agent won't be as interested if their client cannot produce a good proposal. Usually it's better to seek an agent once the proposal has been somewhat developed. Agents can help you get a better deal and often can break through to the editors better that you can because they have established relationships.

Chapter Five
Legal Issues: Agents, Contracts, and Copyrights

"Writing is the painting of the voice."

Voltaire

Just like other art forms, writing deserves to be protected from plagiarism and copying. It has taken me years to learn the ins and outs of contracts, how to successfully work with agents, and what copyrights are about. In order to safeguard your experience and make it as rewarding as possible, there are some nitty-gritty issues that many people prefer not to discuss that should be carefully considered. Even though this chapter is situated at the end of this book, many of its contents should be given serious thought before beginning your book.

Agents can be extremely helpful when writing and selling your cookbook. If you work with a literary agent, you will need to first pitch them your idea (and yourself) before beginning a working relationship. Because the idea of "pitching" yourself and your manuscript more than once is daunting, many people skip this step and attempt to submit their work straight to an editor themselves, or choose to self-publish. Honestly speaking, it can take exactly the same amount of time to hear back from an agent as it takes to hear back from a publisher. Good agents are also just as selective as publishing houses are.

Why then, you may wonder, is it worth taking the time and trouble to attract an agent? Well, for starters, agents know the publishing world like no one else. They have long-standing relationship with many companies, and a keen sense of who is looking for what and when. Since it is their job to sell book ideas, they do it very well. Some publishing companies will not accept "unsolicited manuscripts," so without an agent, you can't even approach them. In addition, agents can help you negotiate the best contract terms and advance on royalties. Building a relationship with an agent enables you to focus on what you do best (which is hopefully, write and cook) and leave the rest to the professionals. In return for their efforts, agents usually earn 15 percent of the advance total from your book. So, for example, if you earned a $20,000 advance, your literary agent would charge you $3,000.

I know, respect, and have worked with many literary agents. As luck and destiny would have it, however, I have sold all of my books on my own. That is partly because I have a large network of contacts, and partly because I was approached as a subject matter expert to write some of my books by publishers directly. If that is not the case for you, I would strongly consider finding and hiring an agent. In fact, I have just begun collaborating with Clare Pelino (see her tips on Coaching on a Cookbook Proposal) on some future books. We have a fantastic synergy, and she understands my work and my goals well.

It is important for your working relationship that the agent you select works with your book genre. Even within the cookbook field there are many niches. Some people represent healthy/self-improvement type books, while others prefer more scholastic books, and others still might like trendy food finds. Take a look at the other authors that your prospective agent is representing. If they are similar to you but offering different types of material, that is a good match. You also want to make sure that the types of books those authors are putting out would be appreciated by your demographic. If the agent typically represents agents who help authors produce books on cake pops, popsicles, and hamburgers, and your book is on the regional cuisine of a particular ancient country, you are probably not a good match. But if the person represents "similar but different" authors and projects, you are probably a great match. The next step is to contact them, write a brief note introducing yourself, and include your bio and proposal. Then you can suggest a brief phone call and take the rest from there.

My friend, colleague, and award-winning cookbook author Nancy Baggett has provided some additional tips here:

The Role of the Literary Agent
By Nancy Baggett

Many editors and writers (myself included) think that having a literary agent is a good idea. Experienced agents are familiar with literary contracts and standard publishing industry practices. So, they are usually better able to negotiate advantageous deals and avoid common legal pitfalls than general practice attorneys. I've often found that agents actually earn their commission by negotiating for better terms than I'd have gotten for myself and by putting me on to opportunities I'd have never have known about without them. Another advantage of agents: They handle the money matters and any editorial problems with the editor, allowing the author and editor to maintain a cordial relationship and concentrate on the task of producing the best book possible.

Unfortunately, it's often challenging to find literary representation. The key reason—a hard business reality—is that most reputable literary agents (as opposed to scammers) only make money when they sell manuscripts. They get paid a percentage—usually 15 percent—of whatever their author gets paid. If they pluck a promising query package from the ever-expanding submissions pile, then spend months (or years) helping the author polish it, but never sell it to a publisher, they go uncompensated for their time. They may end up with a grateful writer, but that pays no bills. And according to a former agent friend (now retired), the "reward" is sometimes blame that the manuscript didn't sell. Little wonder that many agents are quite cautious about unknown quantities and queries that come in unrequested, or "over the transom" as the lingo goes.

Having a published writer who likes your work introduce you to an agent can be very helpful in getting at least a foot in the door. And, any published writing you have already or evidence of a significant media platform will help show a literary agent you are worthy of at least a preliminary look. Attending writing conferences and taking workshops on how to write a tempting pitch letter and book proposal is another excellent step. (Agents are mostly interested in proposals rather than completed manuscripts. They want a hand in shaping material to be sent to publishers.)

A well-written and carefully thought out submission from you to an agent is the strongest possible evidence that you have the skills to do the book. Sometimes, conferences even provide opportunities to meet and chat with agents and editors. Be sure you have a short, very professional elevator speech prepared. And if you're greeted with enthusiasm, ask for a business card and offer to send the agent a book proposal package. Always be courteous; it's important to leave a positive impression with anyone you wish to work with in the future. See the excellent site AgentQuery for lots of additional info as well to find a vetted list of agents.

LEGAL ISSUES: AGENTS, CONTRACTS, AND COPYRIGHTS

Contracts

If you are working with a traditional publishing house, you will be given a contract for your book. It is extremely important to the success of your book (and in maintaining your own sanity while writing it) that you make sure that you are agreeing to terms that you understand and can uphold. If you are working with a literary agent, they will help you to understand the contract and negotiate terms with the publisher if necessary. If not, I strongly suggest investing in the assistance of a lawyer specializing in the publishing industry. Some of the internet sites named in the Suggested Reading/Resources section such as AuthorGuild.org actually provide legal consultation services to members. Whichever option you choose, make sure that you are familiar and comfortable with all of the terms before signing the agreement.

Your contract, publishing agreement, or author agreement will contain the date it was created, your name and address, and the publisher's name and address. It will also tell the tentative title of the book, which will be referred to as "the work." One of the major components of the agreement is to outline the responsibilities of the author and the publisher. It will give specific instructions on how to submit the material, font-size, type of document, etc.). There is also a section which explains the rights of the author and the publisher in terms of the title of the book, copyrights, and rights to translate the book into other languages. If you know, for example, that you would like to have your book translated into a particular language and sold in a country that your publisher currently does not do business in, it is a good idea to have a "Right of First Refusal to (insert language here)" translation. This can give you the opportunity to translate and sell the book on your own, elsewhere, if you know that there is a market for it. Keep in mind that adding this clause, or making any significant changes, can increase the time it takes to complete the contract.

The contract also contains a "Warranties and Representations" section which explains your responsibilities to provide original work, that does not infringe on other copyrights. There is also an indemnification clause which explains that you will hold the publisher harmless if there are any lawsuits or problems arising from copyright infringement. The contract will state that it is your responsibility as the author to obtain written permission from a publisher prior to reprinting any material from another author.

Another section of the agreement which is extremely important is the "Compensation" portion. This shows how much of an advance against royalties (the amount you will be paid to write the book) and the percentage of author royalties that you will receive after selling a certain number of copies. It will state when the publisher shall report sales (usually bi-annually) and when royalties are paid. It also tells you how many complimentary copies of the book that you are entitled to and what your author discount for purchasing books will be.

Spend extra time reviewing the "Submission and Production" portions of the contract, because these are literally the template for your book creation. These sections outline when and how to submit your work. If you think that you may need extra time to complete certain chapters, it is good to state that up front. It is better to give yourself more time than to miss a deadline. Check your personal and professional calendars prior to committing to the dates in the contract. This portion also gives the publisher the right to edit, and explains the terms for delivering work and the publisher's review process.

My cookbook mentor, Sheilah Kaufman, whom this book is dedicated to, always told me, "If you want to write, you have to love to edit, because you will spend more time editing than writing." She is correct. The contract will explain the different stages of editing, typesetting, and corrections. Procedures vary from company to company, but most professional publishers will have your book go through multiple rounds of edits (and for good reason) before sending it to the printer.

Nowadays, most agreements also contain a non-competition clause, which will ask that you agree not to write, edit, print, or publish a work which is competitive to the title that this agreement refers to for at least two years. If you are currently working on a similar project, it is best to disclose the information up front. Even though I have written multiple cookbooks, this clause has not yet been a problem for me because the books I write within the immediate future are different enough to be considered non-competitive. There is usually also an "Option for Next Work" section in which the author is asked to submit to the publisher your next work if it is a competing title. If they do not want to publish the work, after a certain amount of time specified in the contract, you will be able to sell it elsewhere without infringement upon the non-competition clause.

Marketing and design are very important features of your book. In most cases, the final decision is always granted to the publisher in standard contracts. If you have specific "deal breakers" in terms of photography, aesthetics, design, and marketing, this is the place to spell those out. One of the questions that I get asked the most is about photographs and the procedures surrounding them. I have had vastly different experiences with various publishers, so it is hard to give a one-size fits all rule to go by. What I can say, however, is to spend as much time talking about this aspect as you see fit. Make sure that the publisher has a clear idea of your vision in terms of photography or other images or design elements, and that you understand theirs. They may have a standard mode of operation which could be detailed here, or you could negotiate something specific. I have had personal experiences where I was explained the photography procedure upon the signing of a contract (where they were not detailed), and then ended up having a completely different experience with the book than what I expected. In order to avoid problems, it's best to work out the quirks in the beginning. My personal preference for cookbook photographs is when the publisher contracts professional and well-respected photographers, stylists, and chefs to work with your book, and they allow the author to be present at the photo shoot.

Food photographers and food stylists are two totally different things, each worthy of their own salary, that contribute to the overall quality of the book. A professional chef is important as well. Some stylists have chefs already working on the team. They follow your recipes and cook them to perfection, keeping in mind the needs of the food stylist. This makes a huge difference in ensuring that the food looks both appealing, and the way it is supposed to.

In addition to these aspects, there will probably be many other things included in your agreement. Remember that while it is tempting, especially as a new author, to quickly sign an agreement and get the process started, it is beneficial to make sure that the contract is a good fit for both you and the publisher. Most publishers are happy to answer your concerns verbally, on a phone call, and in writing.

Copyrights

Discuss copyright options with your publisher. At times, they will handle the process for you. Consult www.copyright.gov to submit your own paperwork, which you can have a lawyer review. Keep in mind that it takes many months—sometimes a year—to complete the actual registration process, so it is good to get the process started as early as possible. Many publishers will print the books before having the actual copyright registration, and then add it in later. Keep in mind that recipes which are just a list of ingredients cannot be copyrighted. The header of the recipes and your book, however, can. Directions on how to proceed as well as answers to commonly asked questions and a schedule of fees are all located on the copyright office's website.

Chapter Six
Publishing: Self-Publishing vs. Traditional

"We write to taste life twice."

Anais Nin

I often urge readers to consider publishing options before writing their books. The type of platform on which you choose to publish your work could play a role in the type of book that you create. In my career, all of my own works have been published the traditional route. I have also co-written books which were self-published, so I have a little bit of experience there as well. Please keep in mind that even within the "traditional" and "self-published" genres, there is still a lot of variance depending upon which company you end up collaborating with. General rules such as amount of work, creative license, time frames, and marketing/distribution, however, tend to be somewhat similar within each type of publishing.

Before deciding which type of publishing is best for you, it is good to ask yourself:

1. What is my budget to produce a book?

- If you have money set aside to create your book, then the various types of self-publishing would be available to you.

2. Do I need to earn an advance on this book?

- If you are looking to earn an advance for your manuscript and do not have the resources (or do not want to spend them) on self-publishing, then the traditional route might work best for you.

3. Is my topic something that a traditional publishing house would be interested in?

- In order to be successful with a traditional publishing house, you will need to present a proposal for a topic which would enhance their current (and forthcoming) list of books. If your book does not feel like a good fit for various companies, self-publishing would be a better route.

4. Do I have enough of an author platform (see "Chapter Two: Building an Author Platform") to present myself as an attractive prospect to a traditional publishing house?

- Traditional companies want to work with authors who have a proven track record in selling their work. If you can guarantee lots of social media traffic, successful events, and your own PR, you are much more likely to get a traditional contract. Otherwise, read Chapter Two to build your author platform before publishing—regardless of how you plan to do it. It will set you up for success.

5. Do I need to publish this book by a certain date?

- Most self-publishing platforms can put a book out in one to three months' time, whereas traditional publishers take a minimum of nine months, and sometimes years, to release books.

6. Do I have the time/desire to manage the task of publishing in addition to writing my book?

- If not, you need to hire someone to do it for you (for self-publishing), or work with a traditional publisher.

7. Do I have previous publishing experience?

- If so, self-publishing will be easier for you than it is for newbies.

8. Do I want to see my book in bookstores?

- You have a much better chance of getting your book in stores with larger publishing houses. For many people, however, this is not a factor in the success of their overall book.

I highly recommend a website called authorlearningcenter.com, which offers invaluable tips and resources for authors. They offer a standard free trial for thirty days, and have shared with me this promo code—"get45"—which will enable you to get a free 45-day trial at the time of this book's printing (note that the offer may end without prior notice). Known as the "GPS for your publishing journey," there are few publishing questions they do not offer answers to. Among their great variety of information is a chart called *"The Four Paths to Publishing"* written by Keith Ogorek, SVP Marketing at Author Solution and writer of www.indiebookwriters.com. I have quoted his entire article below, but it is worth actually visiting the site to see the additional videos and get more information.

"1. DIY PUBLISHING

DIY is a self-publishing option in which an author uses an upload tool like Booktango (an Author Solutions imprint) or Lulu to create a book and get it into distribution. Some of these solutions may be e-book only or have limited distribution, but if you follow through, you can get your book formatted and available for sale in at least one format and through at least one online retailer. Many of these options are promoted as "free" to publish, but there is a misperception that DIY means you don't have to spend any money. Even if you choose the DIY path, you should still have your book edited, and you will likely have to invest in marketing.

ADVANTAGE: Usually the least amount of financial investment needed to publish a book in at least one format.

DISADVANTAGES: Formats and distribution can be limited. Most options do not have any professional services available, so an author has to find the services needed to complete the project apart from the publishing solution.

2. GENERAL CONTRACTOR

The second option an author can pursue is the General Contractor publishing path. This requires hiring a number of independent service providers such as an editor, book designer, publicist, etc. and coordinating all those activities.

Typically, you will need to obtain quotes from each of the vendors, based on the project, and it will likely require more of a financial investment than DIY. More importantly, if you decide to be your own general contractor, it will definitely take significantly more time to manage the process and coordinate the activities. You also have the option of hiring someone to be your general contractor. That's because, as this option has emerged, a number of people have begun to promote themselves on the Internet as "publishing consultants." They usually have some publishing experience but don't typically offer any services themselves other than helping you find the vendors you need.

Depending on which services you choose and which vendors you use, this option can require the largest financial investment of any of the publishing paths and can take the most amount of time to manage the process.

ADVANTAGE: Select the special individuals who work on every aspect of your book and promotion.

DISADVANTAGES: Can require the most time and money, depending on scope of the project.

SAMPLE LIST OF PUBLISHING TASKS

Write book	Interior design	Print books	Social media
Create title	E-book formatting	Ship books	Publicity
ISBN	Illustrations	Sell books	Events
Copyright or protect	Cover copy	Track royalties	Video interview
Edit	Distribution for print formats	Website	Video trailer
Cover design	Distribution for digital formats		

These are just some of the tasks that are needed to get a book published and promoted, so you want to have a clear idea of how much work you want to do yourself versus having someone else do the work.

3. SUPPORTED SELF-PUBLISHING

The third way that you can get your book ready for sale is to work with a supported self-publishing company whose bundles of services help you get your book and cover designed in print and digital formats, in distribution, and available for sale. In addition, these companies typically offer a full menu of professional services for publishing, promoting, and selling your book. Most of Author Solutions's imprints, including AuthorHouse, Trafford, iUniverse, and Xlibris, fall into this category. The biggest advantage to this publishing path is that it's a one-stop shop for everything that you could possibly need to achieve your publishing goal. Sure, it requires a financial investment, but because there is a range of package offerings and price points, it's apparent from the start what you will get and what it will cost. This transparency is not always possible with the General Contractor path, because you won't know what you will need to spend until you get all of your estimates. Another advantage to the supported self-publishing path is that you typically have only one number to call. In the case of ASI, you have 24/7 customer service available. In addition, you have only one vendor relationship to manage no matter how many services you use. With the General Contractor path, you will likely have multiple vendors, which can take considerably more time to manage.

ADVANTAGE: One-stop shop for everything you need to publish, promote, and distribute your book, and you have selection, service, and convenience.

DISADVANTAGES: Can require more of a financial investment than DIY, and packages may include services that you do not want or need, although some customization is usually possible.

4. TRADITIONAL PUBLISHING

The fourth path, Traditional (or legacy publishing), was the one discussed in the introduction. Historically, if you had a manuscript or book proposal, you needed to find an agent to represent you. Then, he or she would take the project to publishers with the intent to sell it and get an advance against future royalties. Unlike the first three paths, where you retain your rights to the content, on this path you assign the rights to the publisher, so you don't have the same degree of control of your book as you do with the DIY, General Contractor, or Supported Self-Publishing paths. In addition, publishers can take a long time to evaluate, select, and actually publish a book, so you will need to be patient and resilient if this is the only path you want to pursue.

If you do find a traditional publisher who wants your work, you will likely find they can improve it because of their experience and expertise at making books better. They may also have a sales force in place to push certain books to retailers, so you may find support from them that you won't have if you self-publish. However, as a result of the changes we have discussed, many traditional publishers are now looking at self-published books as a source of content that they may want to pick up. In fact, if you watch the headlines, you will see publishers acquiring the rights to titles from all three of the self-publishing paths discussed in this paper.

Chapter Seven
Compiling a Cookbook

"Fill your paper with the breathings of your heart."
William Wordsworth

Finding compelling ways to organize content is one of my favorite parts of the whole cookbook creating process. Cookbooks have come a long way in terms of presentation and layout. Determining a unique layout enables you to set yourself apart from the competition while also reinforcing the overall idea of the book and your personal philosophy.

Up until recently, most cookbooks consisted of a collection of recipes which were organized by category, which was determined by the type of cuisine. So, if you were writing an American cookbook, you would probably start with some acknowledgements, then an introduction, and then chapters based on course, in this case:

- Appetizers
- Soups, Stews, and Chilies (Sometimes pasta gets inserted here, sometimes it is its own chapter. Same goes for salads.)
- Entrees (usually animal/protein-based dishes divided into poultry, meat, game, and seafood categories)

- Side dishes and/or salads
- Desserts

If the cookbook were written about French food, it would have the following chapters:

- Hors d'oeuvres
- First Courses
- Second Courses
- Vegetables
- Desserts

If it were written about Italian food, then it would be organized this way:

- Antipasti (Appetizers)
- Primi (First Courses)
- Secondi (Second Courses)
- Contorni (Side Dishes)
- Insalate (Salads)
- Dolci (Desserts)

In each of these formats, there would sometimes be additional chapters for breads, homemade condiments, and base recipes. Sometimes there would be a glossary or a list of common kitchen utensils or ingredients. The basic premise of the organization, however, left nothing up to the imagination. These are the types of cookbooks many of us grew up with, and there is nothing wrong with organizing a book this way. Actually, sometimes when dealing with complicated recipes or concepts, it is actually beneficial to organize them in a way that the reader is used to.

When I was writing my latest book, *The Italian Diabetes Cookbook*, for example, I chose to present the recipes in the standard Italian format. It wasn't that I didn't want to get creative, but I wanted the focus to be mainly on the content of the recipes (that they were healthful *and* Italian), and also to present the reader who might not have grown up eating in an authentic Italian fashion the way in which Italian meals are actually enjoyed. In addition, the book adheres to the American Diabetes Association dietary guidelines for diabetes-friendly meals which are usually based on an American eating style, so making the recipes adhere to the guidelines while still being appetizing and accurate was already something noteworthy, and I didn't feel the need to introduce additional layers of complexity. These tried but true methods of organization work well for classic books which want to maintain tradition as well as for simplifying complicated concepts and recipes.

With my first books, *Arabian Delights: Recipes & Princely Entertaining Ideas from the Arabian Peninsula* and *Nile Style: Egyptian Cuisine and Culture*, however, I created dramatically different layouts. Because *Arabian Delights* was written in the Arabian Peninsula, a place that many Americans don't have the opportunity to visit, I wanted to use my book to create a platform for the region's culture. So, I created a cultural/culinary format. After the acknowledgements, introduction, and historical overview, I created three separate parts which were then divided into chapters. Part 1 was called "Palatial Feasts," Part 2 was named "Special Ceremonies," and Part 3 was called "Simpler Delights." Each part was then broken down into separate chapters. Special Ceremonies, for example, contained chapters entitled "Yemeni Sabbath Luncheon" and "Ramadan Dinner" to name a few. In each chapter, I gave the cultural and historical overview of the holiday, occasion, or ceremony. Then, I gave a menu for the occasion and all of the corresponding recipes. At the end of each chapter, there was an "Entertaining Timeline" to tie-in to the "Entertaining Ideas" portion of the subtitle, which outlined how someone could recreate one of these festivities in their own home. I had never seen anything done like that before, and believe that this is the best format when introducing a culture to another through food.

Nile Style: Egyptian Cuisine and Culture also has a cultural-culinary format like *Arabian Delights,* but it was slightly different. Because this was the first book to outline Egyptian food in history, I wanted the chapters and menus to be chronologically organized so that the reader could literally travel through time and see how food evolved in the country. Part 1 was "Ancient Festivals," and I started out by recreating a menu from an Ancient Egyptian Nile Festival. The final Part 3 ends with a chapter called "The Revolution: Freedom, Justice, and Bread," and tells my story of being in Egypt during the revolution as well as many authentic and little-known bread recipes. The book opens with a comprehensive, first-of-its-kind Egyptian culinary timeline and ends with a "Where to Buy Guide" and a section on places to visit while in Egypt—so that it could also be used as a guidebook for tourists. I did not create Entertaining Timelines for this book, because the recipes weren't as elaborate and entertaining was not the main focus as it was with *Arabian Delights*. I also did not group the recipes together in categories, as I did with *The Italian Diabetes Cookbook*, because I believed that since this cuisine was lesser known to Americans, it would be more effective to recreate full menus.

When I was asked to write *The Ultimate Mediterranean Diet Cookbook,* I chose to organize the book and its chapters the same way in which the Mediterranean Diet Pyramid is presented. That way, the largest chapter is centered on plant-based foods (which we should be eating the most of) and the smallest chapter is dedicated to Meats and Sweets (which the diet recommends eating very sparingly). I believed that this layout would reinforce the tenants of the Mediterranean Diet and make maintaining the lifestyle easier for readers.

In 2013, Chef Luigi Diotaiuti and I wrote *The Al Tiramisu Restaurant Cookbook: An Elevated Approach to Authentic Italian Cuisine.* The main purpose of the book was to serve as a memoir and also to tell the story of Washington DC's "most authentic" restaurant. We also organized this book chronologically, but instead of starting in the beginning, we started in the present day in the first chapter and then went back to Luigi's childhood in the second chapter and continued to fill in the rest chronologically. Recipes and concepts were organized in accordance with the various times of his life and stages in the restaurant's development, instead of all together at the end.

This way, the reader can truly get a feel for how both the food and the story developed together. This is my favorite way of organizing a memoir cookbook.

As you can see, there are as many ways to organize a cookbook as there are to cook a chicken. It is up to the author to decide which layout will work the best for the reader while underlining the voice and scope of the book. When you are compiling your cookbook, ask yourself the following questions:

1. Is the content of this book so complicated that if I present the content in a new/innovative way, it will confuse the readers?

- If so, stick with traditional formats and use verbiage that is as easy to understand as possible.

2. What are my key messages of the book?

- If one of your key messages is that you are "de-mystifying" a certain cuisine or cooking style, then an easy to follow format is crucial.
- If your key message is that cooking is fun, then the book should be organized in a fun-to-read format.
- If one of your key messages is to tell the culinary history of a place, then a chronological format may be best.
- If you are introducing readers to a cuisine they are not familiar with, how could you lay the book out in order to reinforce the local traditions?

3. If I were the reader, and I may not be very knowledgeable about the topic, what would be the best way for it to be presented?

- Imagine you are a teacher presenting a lesson plan. That type of information should be incorporated into the book.

4. Is this a memoir?

- If so, chronological layouts work well.

5. How would I like to see a cookbook organized?

- There is no right or wrong answer to this question, but if you have a burning desire to see cookbooks organized in a particular way, then that is probably what you should go with—just be sure it matches your content and voice.

Asking yourself some of these questions will help to get yourself on track. If you are unsure of which style to choose, you could write a brief synopsis of each and present it to your friends and co-workers for feedback. Their comments may even provide additional inspiration. If you work with a traditional publisher, they may also have ideas about how your book should be put together. If you are self-publishing, however, the sky is the limit. Enjoy the creative process, knowing that the thought and attention that you invest in organizing your book's content will make a huge difference in the final product.

COMPILING A COOKBOOK

Compilation Tips from Ale Gambini

Food Writer, Italian Food Ambassador, Cookbook Author, Award-Nominee Chef on Online Food Program
Author of *A Queen in the Kitchen, Nonna Fernanda's Authentic Northern Italian Cuisine with a Twist of Me.* www.aqueeninthekitchen.com

As Italian born and raised, Italian Food Ambassador and cookbook author my goal is to spread the authentic Italian cuisine throughout the globe. When writing a cookbook about Italian comfort food, it is very useful to order the chapters following the typical Italian meal structure:

Antipasti (Starters)
Primi (First Course)
Secondi e Contorni (Main Dishes and Sides)
Dolci (Desserts)
Caffe and Ammazzacaffe (Coffee and Liqueurs)

If you are sharing your own family recipes or the ones that grandma handed down to you as in my cookbook *A Queen in the Kitchen, Nonna Fernanda's Authentic Northern Italian Cuisine* with *a Twist of Me*, add to each recipe some anecdotes, a tip or two about how to prepare that dish. Sharing is caring, and when it comes to comfort food, is much more than a recipe. It is the story of your life.

If you are thinking of writing a single-subject cookbook, keep in mind that it could be very challenging. A single-subject book can easily reach readers passionate about a specific subject (pasta, cakes, coffee), but on the other hand, it could turn into a boring reading. You need to be very passionate, unique, and know very well the topic you're writing about because it will be your companion for years. Researching, writing, testing, and eating food related to that topic will be a part of your daily routine.

Nowadays there are tons of chefs, cooks, food bloggers, recipes developers, and food writers eager to write a cookbook. What makes the difference between you and the other writers is your deep knowledge, and your own creativity and personality.

Last but not least, give yourself deadlines; otherwise it will end in another unfinished book.

If you feel you really have something good to share, go ahead and embrace the journey of writing a cookbook. Buona Fortuna and Buon Appetito!

Chapter Eight
Cookbook Promotion

"The destiny of nations depends on how they nourish themselves."

Brillat-Savarin

Planning the promotion of your cookbook is every bit as important as writing it, testing the recipes, and publishing it. Without intensive promotion, it will be very hard for your book to gain recognition, and it will be lost among the thousands of others that our published each year. When working with traditional publishers, the time period from when you give you manuscript to the editor until it gets published is usually a minimum of nine months, which is ample time to begin making promotional plans. If you self-publish, however, you may have a completed book a few weeks to a month after you upload your manuscript, so you will need to plan earlier.

Ways to market your book may include:

Author-Driven Publicity:

Whether you are new or a seasoned writer, you will want to maximize PR for your book. New books garner more attention than many other products, so if you are promoting your personal brand or restaurant, the release of a new cookbook can help to get your business featured in multiple media outlets. If you are extremely well-connected to media contacts, now will be a great time to use them. I highly recommend a professional PR firm that deals specifically with cookbooks to manage planning your launch for you. If you choose to publish your book with a traditional company, they may contract someone to help launch your book for you. If you are self-publishing, it is a good idea to hire someone on your own, even if it is for a short period of time. I recommend:

1. Working with a PR Agent

Whether you are contracting your own agent or working with someone that your publishing company has hired for you, it is a great idea to set up an introductory interview. Let your agent get to know you. Explain your niche and your cookbook goals to them. Let them know any marketing ideas and pre-existing contacts that you have to work with. If you know that your book would fit in perfectly well at a particular event or on a certain show, share your ideas with them. Many people view the agent-author relationship as a one-way street that is driven by the agent. The most successful collaborations come when you work together. A talented agent will know their job responsibilities as well as the intricacies of dealing with the media. You know your work, your book, and your particular areas of expertise. The perfect union would be for you to be readily available to assist them in finding the best market-driven opportunities for your book.

There are many different theories on which kinds of media exposure are the most beneficial. I believe that all exposure is good for your book and for your brand. In the olden days, if you made a television or radio appearance, the interview was dead once it ended. Same thing for the newspaper or magazines. Once those issues were replaced with new ones, your article would be forgotten, unless you cut it out and framed it. Nowadays, with the internet, you can get a link for TV appearances and magazine and newspaper articles, which, if you plan correctly, can be almost "evergreen" in the life of the promotion of that particular book. I always choose to contribute and prepare recipes which I know have a long "shelf-life," so that I can use them to promote the book in the future.

2. Creating a Press Release

A well-written and well-placed press release will help you and your book get the attention it deserves. If you have a PR agent, they will craft and post a press release, with your approval, on the press wire. This will ensure that it gets delivered in a professional manner to all major media outlets. Nowadays you can even specify which regions and professional categories that you would like to receive your release. If you are working on your own, you could pay someone for an "a la carte" type press release service in which you would pay them to write and post the release alone instead of contracting them on a monthly or semi-annual basis. For this option, I currently recommend PRWeb.com. Their website offers a multitude of options, and I have used them with great results on several non-book related occasions.

3. Social Media

Social media is an extremely valuable tool for marketing your book. I know that there are many people who believe that social media is a waste of time, but I don't know any best-selling authors who feel that way. In my personal career, social media has enabled me to document my work and promote my cookbooks in a personal and interactive way. I love the way that I am able to respond to my readers' concerns, questions, and comments so quickly thanks to Facebook, Twitter, Instagram, and YouTube. Pinterest is also really worth your while, even though the interaction is often less than it is on the other platforms.

In my career, my social media posts have enabled me to:

- Sell more books than I would be able to do without it
- Explain my philosophy/brand to followers and consumers

- Be invited to book fairs around the world
- Write numerous magazine columns
- Be an invited speaker at seminars
- Write other books
- Teach courses all over the world
- Form powerful business partnerships
- Get rapid and fast exposure in new genres and reach demographics that I did not previously have access to
- Be included in important culinary and cultural events
- Prove that cookbook writing is a career to be taken seriously

One of the reasons so many practical people don't like using social media to promote their businesses is because there is a belief that you cannot easily correlate posts with the direct sales of your book. To be frank, however, if you add up all of your followers on each platform which you post on, you will know that each post pertaining to your book will be viewed by a minimum of that many people. So, if you have a combined total of 10,000 people following/friending you, and each day you post something compelling about your book, you can rest assured that at least those 10,000 people see it. Once people begin to share your content, that number grows. I feel it is worth it. Sometimes I post links to television shows or appearances I'll be making, and my agents will track to see if there is an increase in sales on Amazon, and there always is. In Italian, we have a saying—*"tutto fa brodo"*—which literally translates as "everything makes broth" and means "every little bit counts." And so it is with social media.

I suggest the following:

1. A YouTube Channel

- Create videos with introductions to your books as well as recipe videos. You can also upload clips from your appearances here. It is the best way to bring your books and recipes to life, and you can use these videos on your other social media platforms.

2. A professional Facebook Page (or two, or three!)

- Create a supporting Facebook page for the book, where readers will be able to find extended resources, up-to-date information, and can discuss with the authors and other users via an online forum. The site will also include a blog, podcast, and speaking engagement calendar. One great post a day is sufficient.

- In addition to the book page, you will want to reference the book on your professional and personal pages as well. Some authors have groups or are part of groups which encourage posting of recipes—this will help to expand your reach. If it is permitted, post recipes which will be relevant to the group's needs. For example, I have three pages in addition to my own on Facebook. One of them is called "The 30-Day Mediterranean Diet Resolution," which was a contest I started to promote the Mediterranean lifestyle. The contest is over, but the dialogue is still going strong. I encourage other authors to post Mediterranean lifestyle-friendly recipes and ideas there.

- Leverage Google AdWords, where you can drive users to the Facebook page.

3. Twitter

- Utilize Twitter for ongoing promotional purposes, where you can engage readers and announce book updates and speaking engagements.

- This platform is also perfect for promoting and sharing new research, trends, and "food news" related to your topic.

- Be sure to use appropriate hashtags and try to tie your tweets into "trending" topics. Multiple daily tweets are recommended.

4. Blogs

- Create your own blog. When I first started, my editors insisted I have a blog. I was hesitant, because the blogs that I liked recounted the tales of beautiful dream worlds—a literary escape that I did not see myself as having the ability to offer to readers! They worked with me, though, to determine how I could best translate my niche into a blog, and I have never looked back. My blog is all about sharing "history, culture, and nutrition through global cuisine." I use it as another bridge between me and my readers, and as an opportunity to explore my world and my ideas. Sometimes I post recipes from my books, grouped together for specific holidays or events. I then use the blog post as my daily content for my social media accounts. That way, even though I am providing readers with "free recipes" as some would call them, I get the benefit of having new readers and correspondence. A few well-received blog posts per month can go a long way.

- I also recommend collaborating with other bloggers. You can offer a "book ambassador" incentive to A-list bloggers to host giveaways and contests with your cookbook on their blog. Begin forming relationships with synergistic bloggers as soon as possible.

5. Instagram

- This platform is very popular with editors. Here you'll want to follow all like-minded chefs and authors as well as the media outlets you hope to be featured in. I opt for multiple posts daily. Obviously, pictures are paramount here, and I find that "food porn" and "action shots" are the most popular. If you are not already familiar with the concept of hashtags, you will want to learn about them for both Instagram and Twitter.

6. Pinterest

- Some say that Pinterest is the fastest growing social media platform. Even if it were just "one of the fastest growing," it would still be worthwhile. In addition to being highly addictive, it is great for marketing your books. Be sure to create a professional page with boards dedicated to your own work—both recipes and books—as well as other food and lifestyle related content. Create a specific board for your book and other boards with book categories such as "appetizers," and make sure to include your website, name of the book, and link to purchase the book on the top of your page and in each post. You don't need to pin daily, but once you start, it will probably be hard not to!

7. A Newsletter

- I highly recommend a newsletter for all chefs and cookbook authors. Mine has gotten me many gigs—and helps me to effectively promote my books, classes, and tours. Monthly newsletters are a great way to keep in contact with your readers and followers. While they do take work and planning, it pays off. I feature recipes from my books each month (with appropriate holiday and seasonal themes), as well as purchasing information. I also list my calendar of appearances and classes and any noteworthy PR that I received the previous month. I share recipe videos and recommendations for the work of colleagues as well. Make sure to create a link from your website which enables visitors to sign up for your newsletter.

8. Plan Your Own Media Tour

- Nowadays media tours are reserved for a very small number of top-tier authors. When book tours are not a part of my contract, I plan my own. I work with small, local, and large international venues such as restaurants, cultural centers, wineries, and food companies

- Keep in mind that successful events aren't always the most "likely subjects." In my career, I have had the opportunity to sell books in many large, prestigious places such as The Library of Congress's National Book Festival and the Bibliotecha Alexandrina in Alexandria, Egypt. The two events where I *sold* the most books, however, were at a Mediterranean market called Tastings Gourmet in Annapolis, Maryland, and at an Italian restaurant in my hometown of Jamestown, New York. Moral of the story? No venue is too small or too "unknown." If someone is willing to host you and your book, and you have the time, take the opportunity.

My key to successful promotion is to regard it as one of the most important aspects of my career, while scheduling it as if it were my favorite hobby. I know what it means to my livelihood, and I enjoy it, so I invest time in it. I make editorial calendars for myself, and I recommend that all new authors do the same. Create an excel spread sheet with all of your social media platforms, blog, and newsletter on the left-hand side. Across the top, list the days of the month. Then, on a monthly basis, fill in what your posts will be ahead of time, when possible. I use holidays, special food days, popular hashtags, my own personal inspirations, and trending topics as guidelines. That way, each and every day, all you have to do is look at your calendar and post/write, or schedule posts, in order to have optimal social media exposure. When I say that I schedule promotion as if it were a hobby, I mean that promotion is, by itself, a full-time job if you do it well. Most of us do not have an additional forty hours a week to dedicate to anything. When I plan an event, a book signing, or time to post, I take those out of my "free" time—because many events are unpaid or don't offer the same type of revenue as other aspects of my career. A night spent signing books is every bit as valuable to me as one with family and friends, so I treat them accordingly. For me and many of my colleagues, being a cookbook author is more than a career, it's a lifestyle.

Promotional Tips from Rossella Rago

Host of the *Cooking With Nonna* show and best-selling author

1. Be on social media.

If you want to write a cookbook and aren't on social media already, you should be. Today so much food content is shared through the web, and I've found it invaluable for creating a community of support for any project I'm involved in. There are many forms of social media out there, but for me and my audience, Facebook and Instagram have been the critical platforms—I rarely use any others. Make sure you post often about your book, and be sure to create a hashtag that incorporates your book title and can be used once the book comes out and readers start recreating recipes. Photos are paramount, and handing out a few complimentary books with bloggers and influencers in exchange for beautiful photos of your dishes is always a good thing.

2. Work your contacts.

It is imperative that you create events on your own to publicize your book: book signings, book talks, speaking engagements, cooking demonstrations, etc. Do as many events as you possibly can, and don't be afraid to think outside the box! I once sold seven cases of books at a bagel shop that a good friend of mine owned after she let me do a book signing there. The point is, you never know what is going to be effective, so you should try anything at least once, provided you have the time and resources.

Suggested Reading/Resources

This is a list of websites, resources, and books which can be extremely helpful for both writing and publishing.

AuthorGuild.org

AgentQuery.com

AuthorSolutions.com

Best Food Writing 2016 Edited by Holly Hughes

"Cookbook Corner" column by Amy Riolo in *Entrepreneurial Chef* magazine

CookbookConstructionCrew.com

Indie Book Writers Blog

PRweb.com

Recipes into Type: A Handbook for Cookbook Writers

The McGraw-Hill Desk Reference for Editors, Writers, and Proofreaders

The Naked Truth about Self-Publishing: Updated and Revised Second Edition

The Resource for Food Writers by Gary Allen

Made in the USA
Middletown, DE
27 January 2022